Speaking to the Addictive Personality in the Local Congregation

A GUIDE FOR PASTORS AND PREACHERS

Jay Haug

America is increasingly immersed in an addictive culture. From prescription drugs to alcohol, various eating disorders, and the prevalence of internet porn, more and more people today are mired in life-controlling behaviors they live out in secret and find difficult to overcome. Despite the hopes of many Christians that addictive problems might be less prevalent among the faithful, all the research tells us these problems exist both inside and outside the church.

There are several reasons addicted people will find their way into the church. First, because there remains a cultural perception that "spirituality" offers some help, and an accompanying awareness that addiction has spiritual roots, many people who battle addictive thinking and behaviors find their way into our congregations.

Secondly, in facing the avalanche of internet porn, we might remember what Frederick Buechner said years ago: the spiritual and sexual wires inside our brains are placed near each other and often become cross-wired. Both the spiritual and the sexual have to do with "connection." This is why they are often mixed up in human experience. Many who struggle today by their own admission were deprived of important, necessary and vital connections with parents, adults and peers, or experienced abuse in these relationships. The "connection" was missed while the "false connection" was formed, creating a lasting wound. The church will always attract people seeking the "God connection," but finding themselves settling for something less.

Furthermore, many same-sex attracted men experienced a father wound now sexualized in adulthood. The result is that many who look for God and healthy human connection can find themselves caught in sexual sin, reliving or re-enacting the false but familiar connection. For them, the false connection delivered instant relief but long-term despair. These often unaddressed deep wounds inhibit many people from finding their way to freedom, despite seeking it for decades.

Thirdly, churches and Christian communities are often the first touch between pastors or Christian leaders and addicts of all stripes. The opportunity to gain resources for help and healing from addictions is one church leaders increasingly must acquire, particularly as addiction increases among us. (See end notes)

All of this has created a **kairos** moment for the church, a crisis/opportunity of profound significance, one we can either meet or miss. The question is: do we have a transformative message and personal ministry that can speak to the hunger and thirst of the addictive soul?

Many years ago as a young Episcopal priest, I decided to show the famous "Father Martin" Chalk Talks on alcoholism at my parish in Massachusetts. The films were informative, humorous and engaging. One night, "Freida" (not her real name), came into the sanctuary and literally fell over the back pew and into our lives. This began a long and circuitous relationship that ended with her getting sober after 15-20 years of severe alcoholism. She became an active church member and believer, changed forever by that one event of walking through our doors and the personal ministry that followed. Today, many addicts are not so visible to the eye and the Freidas of the world may not be so obvious. But their numbers are growing, particularly as a pervasive culture makes in-roads to our souls and has easier access to our addictive leanings.

The question before us is how can the church and the Christian gospel speak into the lives of addicts? And is there really any difference speaking to the average church member and an addict with a specific problem? Our answer is "no." In his well-known book **The Return of the Prodigal Son,** Henri Nouwen writes,

"Addiction" might be the best word to explain the lostness that so deeply permeates society. Our addictions make us cling to what the world proclaims as the keys to self-fulfillment: accumulation of wealth and power; attainment of status and admiration; lavish consumption of food and drink, and sexual gratification without distinguishing between lust and love. These addictions create expectations that cannot but fail to satisfy our deepest needs. As long as we live within the world's delusions, our addictions condemn us to futile quests in "the distant country," leaving us to face an endless series of disillusionments while our sense of self remains unfulfilled. In these days of increasing addictions, we have wandered far away from our Father's home. The addicted life can aptly be designated a life lived in "a distant country." It is from there that our cry for deliverance rises up."

What is this crie de couer? Is it Frederick Buechner's "magnificent defeat", the necessary overthrow of the soul by its Creator from the alienating and dominating influence of its enslaving passions? Perhaps people are unaware of any need to be captured by God's living presence as a solution to what ails them. Could it be that our various addictions leave Him no room until they have run their course and our heart cries out for relief? This we know. Many sitting in our congregations wrestle with these secret struggles. Apparently, God's people have long been similarly troubled. As Proverbs 5:14 states,

> "I was at the point of utter ruin in the
> assembled congregation."

Unfortunately, some Christian thought leaders teach that Christians are immune from such things or that their only problem stems from failing to appropriate some important theological truth. Others teach that a crisis experience of some kind or another will wipe the problem away in an instant. But to believe that Christians are ipso facto immune is to be self-deceived and to miss the kairos moment now upon us. The wake-up call, seen through the flood tide of addiction, is here. To admit that the presence of the Risen Savior and his life-changing gospel cannot reach to the parched land of the thirsty soul both inside and outside the church is to betray the gospel we say we believe and to deny God's present power in the life of his people. The thirst for freedom in our human hearts is calling us to go deeper, to rediscover the gospel's power in an addictive age.

If Nouwen is right, then addiction is simply defect taken to extremes, the soul handed over to a stronghold, a pattern often carved out in childhood through abuse or neglect or simply the result of our own personality bent lived out over decades. So in this sense, we are all addicts and if the church can speak to addicts, it will speak to the rest of us who are immersed in this addictive culture that desires to claim us. In this regard, we are all the children of Cain.

[6]Then the Lord said to Cain, "Why are you angry? Why is your face downcast? [7] If you do what is right, will you not be accepted? But if you do not do what is right, sin is crouching at your door; it desires to have you, but you must rule over it." Genesis 4:6-7

Why are addicts and non-addicts essentially the same? It is very simple. As Jesus teaches in the Sermon on the Mount and the 12 Steps drive home, we all are the possessors of character defects. In the parable of the Pharisee and the Publican (Luke 18:9-14), Jesus demonstrates the folly of failing to see one's own character defects while focusing on other people's. "I thank you, Lord, that I am not like other people..." The Pharisee, occupied with the behavior of another, is the poster child for spiritual blindness. Yet, how many of us have read this parable and taken the message away, "Thank you Lord that I am not like the Pharisee?" !! Such is our self-deception about our own on-going character defects.

Speaking personally, one of the most difficult things for me to see about myself has been how obsessing over other people's need to change is almost always the result of my own pride, self-obsession and control. This attitude is demonstrated in self-centered views that others or the world needs to change to fit my preferences, likes and dislikes. Call it ego, pride or self-deception, this and other character defects (sin patterns) create the dis-ease to which addictive behavior offers only temporary relief, as well as negative consequences.

A good definition of addiction is that it is "control run amok." The lure of any addiction is its immediate removal of discomfort or the indulging in momentary pleasure. Mood control is the sought after state. Not every person in our congregations is an addict in the strictest sense. But all humans are plagued by character defects of one kind or another, the same ones the addict attempts to control through medication. For addicts and non-addicts, our true spiritual growth lies in progressive freedom from these character defects.

Reading Matthew 5-7 the other day, I counted 26 character defects mentioned by Jesus. They include anger, fear, lust, pride, revenge, hypocrisy, greed, anxiety and the list goes on. For the addict, these defects are normally the drivers of addiction. They create the agitation and unsettled feeling for which the addiction supplies temporary relief. This then becomes a reinforcing cycle of vice with defect sparking addictive behavior and vice-versa.

For the non-addict, defects create discord, trouble, broken relationships and ultimately despair. Rather than finding a way to surrender these, we often plead the grace of God and forgiveness and then go on about our way until the next flare up. It is one thing to think this is the best we can do. It is quite another to think this is all we can do. Spiritual progress becomes elusive. This problem of stunted spiritual growth is discussed at length in Dallas Willard's helpful book, **The Divine Conspiracy**.

Accordingly, those of us who do not identify as addicts are still faced with the destructive consequences of our character defects. Examples are everywhere: the family member who refuses to speak to a relative due to long-held anger, the greedy employee who secretly embezzles his employer, the prideful organizational leader who controls others and keeps the focus on himself, the husband who finds a younger woman, rather than work through issues with his wife, the fearful woman who finds it difficult to trust others and lives apart as a critic of all she surveys. We might not call these addictions. But they have wounding negative consequences nonetheless. People are hurt and damaged. Relationships are broken, sometimes permanently. God and his way of life are edged out and the promise of the liberty of the sons and daughters of God lies unfulfilled.

An older Christian recently confided in me as follows: "I used to think that if Christians took over the world, it would be a better place. I don't believe that any more. I think it would be just as messed up as it is now." He is referring to what I call "the rude awakening." It happens to people somewhere between a week and never after they come to Christ. The rude awakening looks something like this: "Despite my faith and everything God has done in my life, I still have major problems, some of which I would never confess even to my Christian friends. I am not fixed and I don't really know if I will ever be." Of course, if the truth be told, some in the church believe admitting this problem is tantamount to heresy. Could it be that part of the plague of loneliness in the Christian community today is that we are all suffering from similar problems but nobody is talking about what really ails them? In any case, in many lives there emerges an inner, pervasive and undeniable despair about ever changing, ever walking in freedom and ever knowing real and authentic joy. If recovering alcoholics could become "happy, joyous and free," what about ordinary Christians?

I recently spoke to a friend of mine who has experienced a profound and lasting transformation out of a horribly addictive lifestyle into a close and intimate walk with the Lord. Like all of us, he is not perfect. But he is remarkably happy joyous and free. While taking daily steps to surrender any return to his previous life, he embraces his new life with a thankful heart. My friend has also taught a Sunday School class in a large church for a number of years. He told me with pain in his voice about several people in the class who seem unable to confront or even recognize any struggles or difficulties they have experienced since their initial salvation experience. They seem to have no need of the Lord's presence in their current lives, much less His power in their present weakness. When asked about spiritual things, they look back, rather than to any vitality in their present walk with God or any future hope. My friend is genuinely sad about this lack of authenticity in some church people he sees. He wonders if they will ever desire more. Perhaps they secretly do.

My old teacher Frank Lake use to say that sadly "many people attend church for their defensive purposes." In other words, they present lives that are strong and right, needing little from anyone else, let alone God. Church for them is a place to display talent or simply adequacy and self-sufficiency, rather than a place to admit vulnerability and allow the Lord or others to serve them at their point of need. Sometimes this masquerades as spiritual maturity. The Apostle Paul confronted this same spirit in Corinth.

"8Already you have all you want! Already you have become rich! You have begun to reign—and that without us! How I wish that you really had begun to reign so that we also might reign with you! 9For it seems to me that God has put us apostles on display at the end of the procession, like those condemned to die in the arena. We have been made a spectacle to the whole universe, to angels as well as to human beings. 10We are fools for Christ, but you are so wise in Christ! We are weak, but you are strong! You are honored, we are dishonored! 11To this very hour we go hungry and thirsty, we are in rags, we are brutally treated, we are homeless. 12We work hard with our own hands. When we are cursed, we bless; when we are persecuted, we endure it; 13when we are slandered, we answer kindly. We have become the scum of the earth, the garbage of the world—right up to this moment." I Corinthians 4:8-13

Paul could see right through the Corinthian's façade, directly into their empty and hungry souls. He had discovered God's power and presence through his own defeat and weakness and he wasn't ever going back to the self-righteous, "right and religious" man he was before. If we could just get inside Paul's mind and experience the reality and power of the following passage, we might be onto something.

"Therefore, in order to keep me from becoming conceited, I was given a thorn in my flesh, a messenger of Satan, to torment me. [8] Three times I pleaded with the Lord to take it away from me. [9] But he said to me, "My grace is sufficient for you, for my power is made perfect in weakness." Therefore I will boast all the more gladly about my weaknesses, so that Christ's power may rest on me. [10] That is why, for Christ's sake, I delight in weaknesses, in insults, in hardships, in persecutions, in difficulties. For when I am weak, then I am strong." 2Corinthians 12: 7b-10.

We just might see that God is after something in our weaknesses, addictions and character defects and troubles. He wants us to see his power to turn and use our very weakness as a force in our own lives and with other people. Can the average Christian appropriate this experience of strength through weakness or are we condemned to devastating consequences when our character defects "bring forth death?" (James 1:15)

What if things could be different in the Christian community? Can we become a people who in the right context admit our bondage to one another? How did the early church live out James's admonition to "confess your sins to each other and pray for each other that you may be healed." (James 5:16) I want to believe that most people who walk into church are looking for real and enduring answers for their personal and present struggles, a message that can speak to their agony of soul and make them new.

Many of us do not recognize how powerless we are over these deep seeded defects. Even though we say it in many of our church prayers.

"Almighty God, you know that we have no power in ourselves to help ourselves: Keep us both outwardly in our bodies and inwardly in our souls, that we may be defended from all adversities which may happen to the body, and from all evil thoughts which may assault and hurt the soul; through Jesus Christ our Lord, who lives and reigns with you and the Holy Spirit, one God, for ever and ever. Amen."

(The Book of Common Prayer, Collect for the Third Sunday in Lent, Year B)

The problem is that these evil thoughts have not only assaulted the soul but taken up residence there. Most of us would have sent these problems away long ago if we could. But they persist. Lust, anger, jealousy, anxiety, fear, resentment, resignation, despair. These are the daily struggles pastors, preachers and Christian leaders are called to not only confront in their own lives but to address in their communities of faith. These are the agonies of the soul seeking relief. I am more convinced than ever this is the place in people Jesus wants to speak to and dwell in.

A few years ago, following a difficult period in my own life, I had an extremely vivid dream. At the time, I was sure the dream was descriptive of my current state. Only later on did I realize it was a prophetic look-ahead to God's future action in my life.

I was standing on the edge of a deep river, on a high bluff above a gorge. I was leaning back over the river, hanging on to a substantial tree stump. An important religious figure in my life was standing nearby watching. In the moment, I had not realized that the stump I grasped tightly had rotted through to its core. Suddenly, the stump snapped, sending me cascading backwards over the bank and down toward the water. The feeling of falling was palpable. After what seemed like too long, I finally landed backward in the river and sank all the way to the bottom, at least fifty feet down, whereupon I pushed off and just barely returned to the surface, gasping for breath. I felt reborn, as if the whole world was new and that life had given me a second chance.

It strikes me that this experience of having the rotten core of my character defects exposed and setting forward their inevitable consequences is exactly what the preacher's calling is. Similarly, setting forth what God is up to in our powerless moments, when we are falling and all seems lost, is also the preacher's task, one designed so that new life can break forth all around us.

The vital question is: are we speaking into these kinds of wounds, the real places people live? And how in the world do we speak to them? I believe God's eternal life dwells in the crossroad between Bible passages/kingdom principles and broken human experience. This is what the "sermon is about." Declaratory and propositional messages cannot themselves be transformative without addressing the inner struggles, character defects and sin patterns all of us confront daily. When Doctor Bob, an incorrigible alcoholic met Bill W. and his life was permanently changed, he was asked, "Why now?" After all, Dr. Bob had spent significant time in the Oxford Group. which eventually was turned off by "all these drunks" and then passed into history. He said it was simple. He said he had heard all the principles before. Dr. Bob said, "What Bill brought was himself." The touchstone of human experience applied to the eternal gospel is what changes lives.

Before we move to how we might communicate the gospel in an addictive culture, we need to comprehend two very important principles that proceed from the idea that transformative truth is always filtered through human beings. This is as old as the disciple imitating his master. (sometimes to the last detail! See end notes)

The first principle is that of the 'wounded healer" as articulated by the Apostle Paul in 2 Corinthians 1. 3-4.

[3] Praise be to the God and Father of our Lord Jesus Christ, the Father of compassion and the God of all comfort, [4] who comforts us in all our troubles, so that we can comfort those in any trouble with the comfort we ourselves receive from God.

Those who have received God's comfort from whatever problems, troubles and issues they have faced are the best ones to comfort others with those same problems. In Jesus case, since he has born the sins of the entire world, past present and future, he is able to understand, identify with and redeem everyone's sin.

The Lamb's blood has been shed, but it still needs to be applied to the lintels and doorposts of particular houses and individual lives. How do we participate in his redeeming work in the lives of people facing unique problems? In our highly specific human lives, none of us experiences every problem or addiction or confronts every part of the human condition. Paul is telling us that the way God works is often very particular. When we experience a specific problem and have been comforted (found rest/relief from it), we are called to take that same comfort to those who struggle as we do. We become wounded healers, bearing the very medicine we ourselves have consumed.

The second and related principle is the power of like-problem ministry.

The isolation of human experience is expressed well in the old Negro spiritual.

> Nobody knows the trouble I've seen
> Nobody knows but Jesus

We can easily think we are the only ones battling our specific problems. But why was it that Dr. Bob found liberation through Bill W. sharing his life with him? It was because their root problem of alcoholism was the same. Furthermore the "solution" was available to both. If it worked for Bill, it could work for Bob. One of the necessary callings of pastors in a addictive culture is to help suffering people find their way into like-problem groups, either inside or outside the church. (A fuller discussion of this lies beyond our subject here.)

As pastors, preachers and teachers, we must create the atmosphere for this kind of ministry to take place. To meet the addictive challenge the church faces today, we are called to enter the inner lives of hearers to meet them at the point of their need. A large problem churches face today is that in the minds of wide swaths of the public, the preacher is too often answering questions no one is asking. We are asked to become religious before the human connection is established.

Unfortunately, many preachers and Bible teachers expect listeners to make the inner connection between their struggle and the Biblical text on their own. In effect, they expect the hearer to design his or her own sermon illustration, as the preacher wanders through 1st century Palestine and proclaims what the Bible says. Don't get me wrong. This is far superior than a non-Biblical message. But my experience with what John Stott called 'bridge building," moving back and forth between the biblical world and the world we live in, is that it rarely happens in the listener's mind alone. The result is the stuff that troubles minds and hearts during the week often remains unaddressed on Sunday.

What the average person in the pew needs is someone who understands "the thoughts and intentions of the heart." The book of Hebrews tells us that person is Jesus Christ, the word of God. Scripture tells us, "...he knew what was in man." (John 2:25) In a real sense, the preacher is called to tell us what Jesus already knows and his word already knows about us.

So where do we begin to speak to not just the human condition but to the pervasive addictive culture that surrounds us? How does the preacher/teacher fulfill his or her calling to bring hearers' diseased and laboring souls, into what Hebrews calls a place of "rest."

Hebrews 4:9-13

"9 There remains, then, a Sabbath-rest for the people of God; 10 for anyone who enters God's rest also rests from their works,[a] just as God did from his. 11 Let us, therefore, make every effort to enter that rest, so that no one will perish by following their example of disobedience.

12 For the word of God is alive and active. Sharper than any double-edged sword, it penetrates even to dividing soul and spirit, joints and marrow; it judges the thoughts and attitudes of the heart. 13 Nothing in all creation is hidden from God's sight. Everything is uncovered and laid bare before the eyes of him to whom we must give account."

The addictive soul is desperately looking for a place of rest. Interestingly, this is what Jesus says about impure spirits.

> "When an impure spirit comes out of a person, it goes through arid places seeking rest and does not find it." (Matthew 12:43)

There is neither rest nor water in the desert. Neither is there quenching of thirst through addictive behaviors. The restless soul finds no rest there, unless like Jacob, he finds a rock for a pillow and a ladder to heaven. (Genesis 28:10-15) This is what 21st century people are looking for, even if they cannot articulate it.

How essential it is that the addictive hunger finds its rest in Him. But a place of "rest" can be a several things. It can be a place to stand that replaces flitting about from thing to thing. Stopping is something addicts find difficult to do and need help doing. This place of rest brings clarity. "Rest" can also be a replacement for "works," as God ceased from on the 7th day in creation. In the addictive context, restless souls are trying to fix themselves on their own, or work things out in the darkness alone instead of coming to the fellowship of light. (1 John 1:5-7)

But the burden of our character defects and the laborious task of hiding and defending them, along with ceaseless self-repair is also something from which God desires to give us rest. The law-driven failure expressed in our disobedience (referenced in Hebrews 4:11) and resulting defects creates spiritual turmoil from which our soul seeks rest and an enduring path of freedom.

So how does the preacher/teacher in a parish setting help the people to enter into that rest? Hebrews tells us exactly. It is through the word of God, expressed here as Christ himself, displayed through the written word. This why the writer of Hebrews uses both "he" and "it." Christ is the one who "penetrates even to dividing soul and spirit, joints and marrow; while it (the word written) judges the thoughts and attitudes of the heart." This is the opportunity the preacher/ teacher has to read into the very soul of his or her listeners. This is life-changing spiritual surgery and it takes careful, thoughtful work from someone who knows their own fallen soul, the "thoughts and attitudes" of their own heart. When the human heart is "laid bare" to God's loving and abundant presence and provision, then transformation can truly take place. (I will present a model on how to do this later.)

A Word on the 12 Steps

Those familiar with the 12 Steps will have already made the connection between the terms "addiction" and "character defects" as being taken directly from AA. I am aware that Christians have varying views on the 12 Steps and how they either should be used, not used, or adapted to the Christian gospel.

My view of the matter is simple. I believe that every Christian must have a rule of life. Many Christians fail because their spiritual life is little more than a series of spiritual highs with no connective tissue, no planned growth strategy in place. Every Christian desiring to "grow in the grace and knowledge of our Lord and Savior Jesus Christ" (II Peter 3:18) needs to involve themselves in an intentional process. If not, God's ever deepening character work in us will be truncated. Habitual practice and method work. Without it, we are adrift.

I have found that the 12 Steps work in my life in a transformational manner. They help me confront my deepest issues, adapt needed change, grow closer to God and serve others. It's that simple. There are other rules of life available. Many of them provide this needed structure to further our soul's progress. However, there are many reasons addicted people have found the 12 Steps to be life giving and life-changing.

Secondly, I have not found any programs that adapt the 12 Steps or change them to be more effective. Some Christians are uncomfortable with references to a generic "higher power" in the 12 Steps. Since many of AA's founders were evangelical Christians, we might want to ask ourselves why they did not make belief in God mandatory? Their own explanation was that they did not wish to make faith in God a requirement to join, but rather only a desire to be sober. They also believed that an "authentic spiritual experience" would eventually lead people to that faith. As thousands have found God through AA and its like-addiction groups, this thinking has been proved right.

But there is simply no personal barrier to anyone in recovery making Jesus Christ their higher power. The combination of Biblical Christianity and the 12 Steps has shown itself to be a highly effective combination that can and has brought liberation and permanent change to many. The results speak for themselves.

I do not know exactly how the 12 Steps work., nor do I need to know. Those who first articulated them expressed similar sentiments. The steps simply work when undertaken. They support the truths of the Bible and historic Christian teaching, because they offer a practical pathway for human beings to find freedom and walk in honesty with God and other people and to find both joy and sobriety in service. They enable real change. My hope is that churches will continue to cooperate with and refer their people to healthy groups in their area.

Speaking for Addictive Transformation

So how do we speak to the addictive soul in a congregational setting?. The great Anglican preacher Charles Simeon believed in a very simple manner of preaching which some have abandoned today in favor of proclamation of kingdom principles only. As mentioned previously, there is nothing wrong with this per se, except that the reason we preach and teach is to make room for God to transform his children. The principles we teach may be biblical, sound and true, but unless they are personalized, we will not succeed.

Simeon said his goal was to "humble the sinner, exalt the Savior and promote holiness." But how do we understand this in the light of addictions, character defects and transformation?

To "humble the sinner" is the most difficult task of the three. Human nature is self-satisfied, complacent and bored. And in our entertainment soaked, tickled-ear culture, we demand communication be worth our undivided attention. Our defenses are up and attention spans limited. Many mega churches are defined by two fisted congregants with designer coffee in one hand and smart-phones in the other. How in the world does a preacher/teacher "humble the sinner" in the 21st century and what does that mean anyway?

Remember that we are getting ready to "exalt the Savior." But our listeners are not ready. The Great physician must diagnose before he heals. And hearers must admit "they are sick," or as Jesus said, "They have no need of a physician." It is up to the preacher/teacher to demonstrate and personalize it. Whether people are believers or skeptics matters not. What we have to do is knock our hearers off center by showing them their desperate condition before we get to the good news. If we fail to do this, we will be answering questions no one is asking. Francis Schaeffer used to say that if he had a skeptic in a conversation for one hour, he would spend forty-five minutes on sin. The goal is to create the desire to surrender our defects and our addictions, because we no longer believe they can work for us. After all, if walking with Jesus is just an "option," instead of "bread" and "life" itself, how vital can he be to us?

Do you remember Richard Burton's portrayal of the Roman soldier in the movie "The Robe?" There is one scene I will never forget. Burton's character is in anguish over whether to surrender to Jesus and become a Christian. Another man in the room is in possession of the robe Jesus wore when he was crucified, the one soldiers gambled over at the foot of the cross. At one point in Burton's anguish, the man simply tosses the robe to Burton. At first he reacts as if the robe is cursed and he seeks to get it off him, as a man would to a burning piece of clothing. It is as if he knows what would be required of him should he embrace it. But soon he is overwhelmed by it, clutches it to his breast in agony and then in worship. The old man is finished. The new has begun.

There needs to be something like this in the way we expose the human condition, one that lays bare our need and makes us clutch at the very presence of Christ right where we sit. Then in the loving and gracious reality of Jesus's provision, we turn, surrender and let Him have his way with us. If preachers do this right, our hearers are more likely to respond over time, as both our dire need and Jesus's sufficiency are demonstrated to our hearts. But how do we do it?

Here is a simple outline that demonstrates the kind of model needed. (See end notes) Many passages from the Bible can be adapted to it. I will use John 3:16.

"For God so loved the world that he gave his one and only Son, that whoever believes in him shall not perish but have eternal life."

How do we preach or teach this to addictive people? It might look something like this.

Gospel Demand The wonderful truth of today's word is that God offers us eternal life. This is the ultimate connection we are offered in this world and it is offered by God himself to each of us. What an invitation, to be in relationship with the God of the universe, to know him and His true Son intimately. and to find the hunger of our soul satisfied and its thirst quenched in his daily, hourly presence. Jesus tells us here that he came to establish and maintain that eternal connection with us. It is the reason that he lives today. He longs for relationship with us, one that He designed us for in the beginning. He invites us to turn away from all false connections in favor of the one eternal relationship, the one that satisfies our deepest hunger and thirst both today and for all time.

Sin Behavior But here is the reality in which we often live. Instead of seeking Him, we seek out false connections and false gods. We turn away. As Jeremiah 2:13 says we have "forsaken the fountain of living waters and hollowed out for ourselves broken cisterns that can hold no water." We all know what these broken cisterns are. Money, power, sex and a whole host of other things. When we are agitated, under pressure, bored or lonely we turn to our false connection of choice. Television, internet porn, alcohol, prescription drugs or to the refrigerator to fill us up. We are pros at medicating. We choose the misconnection. We turn away because the reliable quick fix gives us what we seem to need now, every time. We embrace the way of perishing, not the way of life. We may get what will give us temporary relief, but both enduring peace and connection with God slip away. We are losing our freedom, one act at a time.

Illustrations (To break tension and earth these principles in human experience, now is the time for examples, life stories, or additional biblical texts.)

Root Cause Why do we turn away? Why do we forsake the only connection that can bring us life? We turn away because our experience of isolation, fear, anger, resentment and anxiety cry out for instant medication. We are not sure God can fix us now. We often don't believe his promises. Moreover, our sin nature has already found its way to the medicating behaviors of our time. Internet pornography, alcohol abuse, pill popping, eating disorders, excessive screen-time. We have made our choice and practiced it to perfection, constructing deep ruts of negativity into our daily routines. Turning away has become all too easy once our character defects set in. Loneliness threatens us. Anxiety seeps in. Resentment plagues our soul and "the sin that clings so closely" (Hebrews 12:1) seems so appealing and so available. So we indulge, thinking this one time won't be a problem. But it isn't one time. We've done it many times and we are now well practiced. We know the false connection and what it will deliver. We are trapped, lost. Yet we somehow insist we are not perishing. After all, we are saved, right? God will forgive, won't he? Of course. But knowing this can sometimes provide the needed excuse for an addicted mind to continue with our mis-connection. God's presence becomes a distant and shrinking mirage, what someone called "a smudge on the windshield of life." Are we only here to hold onto heaven or is there something or someone who can bring us freedom now?

When Peter was confronted with Jesus miraculous powers in catching fish, he said, "Get away from me Lord. I am a sinful man." Did Peter feel unworthy? No doubt. And sometimes the immediate answer to that feeling of shame is to slip away to a secret place of power and control. In Jesus's presence, Peter's illusion of control was deeply threatened. The open-ended, uncertain calling threatened the old and familiar paths. He would prefer to put distance between him and Jesus.

So, whether we feel unworthy, threatened, or simply want to indulge our misconnection, we turn away, put up our imaginary wall and act out.

Illustrations

We Christians are fond of touting our salvation. Yes, it is by grace we are saved and we believe God is for us, but do we really believe that He is the genuine connection now, one that is worth abandoning our rut of negativity for? Can he save us now? Can he bring eternal life to me now? Can he break this bondage now? We are doubtful. We may believe for other things, but what about for the addictive life that troubles me now? This is where Jesus seeks access, not to blame or accuse, but to heal and set free. He is the ultimate connection, but he wants to be that for us, right now at our point of need and possible misconnection.

Sin Result You see we need a Savior right now, don't we? And if we don't get one in the crucible of our problems in the now, we will continue to abandon the connection with Him. We may go to heaven, but in the meantime we will face some painful consequences before we go. We may lose a spouse or girlfriend, acquire or transmit a disease, go to prison or just slip into isolation, a long depression or an empty, scattered life. At the very least, we will miss out on that liberating connection with God that promises eternal life now, not just at the end, not just in heaven. Without Him, we are in deep trouble. And we know it. Somewhere deep in our souls, something is dying and like the prodigal son, we want to find the way back.

Illustrations

Ok. Now we are getting somewhere with our hearers. They are uncomfortable, agitated, looking for a way out. We have provided real life examples of what they are experiencing. It is only when we have taken them to this place that we have truly "humbled the sinner." He or she knows that you are talking about him or her. They see the pattern. They have walked it and there is something in their lives that relates personally to what you have said. The key here is that you must not move to the gospel until they have felt the pain of their situation and the desperate plight of humans substituting the false connection, instead of what we were created for. We must undermine all possibilities of man's self-sufficiency by outlining its painful consequences and loss of ever being happy joyous and free if we continue down this path. Remember the more we believe the old life still works, the more likely we are to return to it. All the better if the soul is crying out for relief. We should be making our hearers uncomfortable and ready to surrender before we move on.

Now, we turn to the gospel.

The Gospel We now exalt the Savior. Our gospel today has great good news for those of us who find ourselves on the edge, weak, tempted and caught in the web of this world. Jesus tells us that God sent him into the world for us, for these very situations in which we find ourselves. His life is always available to us, in every situation, no matter how tempting or troubling.

For He, Jesus, offers us the real, authentic connection we are looking for. This is what eternal life, a life we can live now, is all about. He spells it out in John 17:3. "Now this is eternal life: that they know you, the only true God, and Jesus Christ whom you have sent." Life that never dies is found in connection and relationship to God himself, shared amongst a community ("they") who know Him and share His life together.

This is the ultimate "connection" the addictive soul is looking for, the only one that brings solid food and thirst quenching drink that satisfies without regret, sorrow or remorse. Jesus said to the woman at the well, "but whoever drinks the water I give them will never thirst. Indeed, the water I give them will become in them a spring of water welling up to eternal life." (John 4:14) He wants to be with us in every trial, every temptation and every difficulty. He desires us to turn to him and surrender every single thing we cannot bear ourselves, as it occurs. The power of freedom comes after I have made the connection with Jesus in the moment and surrendered what I was never meant to bear specifically to him. And the wonderful promise is that he will take it! "Come to me, all you who are weary and burdened, and I will give you rest. ²⁹ Take my yoke upon you and learn from me, for I am gentle and humble in heart, and you will find rest for your souls. ³⁰ For my yoke is easy and my burden is light." Matthew 11:28-29)

Gospel Result

But does it work? Can we really be free of "the sin that clings so closely." (Hebrews 12:1) Yes, we can be, one moment at a time. How can this be? We must first understand the extent to which Jesus has entered our world. Jesus is one who became "fully man." Think about that. We tend to think of Jesus as above it all. Even in his humanity, we think of him as Clark Kent, able to enter the phone booth when necessary and reveal the Superman costume underneath.

But this is wrong. Phillippians tells us that when Jesus came to earth, "…he made himself nothing by taking the very nature of a servant" (Phillippians 2:7) Hebrews tells us "we do not have a high priest who is unable to empathize with our weaknesses, but we have one who has been tempted in every way, just as we are--yet he did not sin. (Hebrews 4:15) This means that Jesus experienced every kind of pull, including sexual temptation, that we have. Did Jesus experience a "pull" from the woman at the well, someone who had attracted six men to live with her? The text does not tell us. But we do know he understands, because Hebrews says he felt every kind of temptation we do. Jesus also felt the full extent of these pulls by never yielding to them. He alone knew their full weight because he surrendered each one to the Father.

Jesus bore the full burden of our fallen selves. In the Garden of Gethsemane, he said, "My soul is overwhelmed with sorrow to the point of death." (Matthew 26:38). The full weight of his approaching sin-bearing death was upon him there. He experienced the full felt consequences of collective human experience, the literal curse of addictive behavior.

"Christ redeemed us from the curse of the law by becoming a curse for us, for it is written: Cursed is everyone who is hung on a pole." (Galatians 3:13) He allowed himself to be overwhelmed and receive the crushing burden of it all. Far from being removed, Hebrews says, "During the days of Jesus' life on earth, he offered up prayers and petitions with fervent cries and tears to the one who could save him from death, and he was heard because of his reverent submission." (Hebrews 5:7)

What is going on here? Why did he do it? Jesus, far from removing himself from the human condition, has entered into it as deeply as anyone ever could. The Apostle Paul tells us that he identified so much with us that He "became sin for us." (2 Corinthians 5:21). Isaiah tells us that the inhumanity of our sin made him "...disfigured beyond that of any human being and his form marred beyond any human likeness." (Isaiah 52: 14) Consider this: There is nothing we have experienced that he cannot look at us and say "I know. I have walked that road myself and I will walk it with you now."

In short, Jesus took our sin and in exchange gifted us with his own birthright, sonship with God the father. In Rembrandt's Crucifixion (1631), the artist painted his own face into Christ's own on the cross. Considered somewhat scandalous at the time, Rembrandt knew how completely Jesus had entered human experience and wanted to portray it. Having lived the prodigal life in his early years, perhaps Rembrandt finally understood that the way back to his father's house was through the cross, embracing the one who embraced his full humanity there.

Because Jesus never "drank" of sin, by surrendering to the Father, he knew the full extent of its power to tempt and draw away from the Father's presence. Then it happened. In one final sin-bearing moment, he experienced an alienation, a drawing away, whose purpose was to end ours, crying "My God, My God, Why have you forsaken me?" (Matthew 27:46) This is a mystery hard to comprehend. But because of his estrangement in that moment from the father, we became the friends of God. Because of the darkness of the cross, the light need never depart from our path. Jesus's surrender invites and empowers ours, in the particular temptation of today. When finally, the temple curtain was torn in two, the very symbol of separation, Jesus gave us access into the very presence of the Godhead, in every temptation we face.

What does this mean for us now? Simply that there is a promise and hope for our moment to moment life now. For he is available to us now, right in the middle of our temptation. "Therefore he is able to save completely those who come to God through him, because he always lives to intercede for them." (Hebrews 7:25.)

We might rightly ask the question, "What is Jesus doing now?" Having sent the Holy Spirit into the world, what does he live for now? Hebrews tells us. He lives to intercede for us.

Here is the way it works for you and me now. Whenever, we are tempted, Jesus, the one who experienced an identical temptation to this very one I am going through now, is present with me holding out his hand, saying "I will take this if you will surrender it to me. I will bear it away." This is the present power of the cross, resurrection, ascension and glorification of Jesus. It is also deeply connected to the thirst-quenching presence of the Holy Spirit promised to all believers, a presence that not only satisfies the believer but also allows him or her to bear the living water of Jesus's presence to others.

⁷ On the last and greatest day of the festival, Jesus stood and said in a loud voice, "Let anyone who is thirsty come to me and drink. ³⁸ Whoever believes in me, as Scripture has said, rivers of living water will flow from within them."[a] ³⁹ By this he meant the Spirit, whom those who believed in him were later to receive. (John 7:37-39a)

The same living water promised to flow into the woman at the well is now promised to "flow from within" those who believe in Jesus to others, quenching their thirst as well. In fact, as the early AA's discovered, they could not stay sober unless they helped others. Just so, Christians find freedom from their own inner struggles by allowing "living water" to flow out to others.

This is the true connection we were meant for and where relief can truly be found. Because we were made with the power of choice, we have the power to keep our temptation, handle it ourselves and refuse to surrender it to him. Or we can respond to his outstretched hand and surrender. It is our decision.

It has taken me a long time to learn that my human instinct to tell God and myself, "I can handle this," dooms me to failure. Instead Jesus wants me to surrender the specific temptation in the moment it occurs. He wants me to admit my utter powerlessness and yield it to Him in the moment. "He lives to make intercession for me." This is his calling, his job, his joy and his crown. And for years, I shut him out, turned away in self-sufficiency and lived in defeat. If there is one principle, one practice, one lifestyle to take from all of this, it is this.

What have I learned about the present power of Jesus in my life? Simply that he will take away any temptation that I give him. Because I am human, and often drawn away, sometimes I have to give it away to him multiple times. But as many times as it comes back, I have learned to give it away to him. He always takes it, if I surrender it. He has never failed. This is not about perfection. It is about learning the daily habit of surrender.

And so, we can live and remain in freedom as we live in Him, one moment at a time, one temptation at a time. This is eternal life and we are called to live in it forever, one day at a time. As we give to others and help other addicts with their struggles, self-seeking and self-centeredness slip away. We begin to comprehend what a life "happy, joyous and free" is all about. This is a "holiness" created by His presence at the very point of human weakness, a process that directly results from surrender and service.

That's it. This is the message. It can be adapted to numerous texts, sermon topics and teaching situations. Please note, none of this is meant to replace needed counseling, therapy and like-addiction groups in church or community. Neither does it deal with working the 12 Steps in detail. It's sole purpose is create a model for Christian leaders to both speak into the addictive crisis upon us and show how Jesus and the gospel provide the ultimate connection for the hungry and thirsty soul and, along with the 12 Steps, provide a way of service to both addicts and other needy souls.

End Notes.

1The purpose of this booklet is to help address the addictive personality in general. Specific help for those involved in porn addiction and other sexual sin is another important challenge that we address at length elsewhere. The church's willingness to explore addictive issues in the open from a gospel and 12 Step perspective is the focus of this booklet.

2 I am grateful to Milton Crum, homiletics professor at Virginia Theological Seminary for this model. It contains far more power and ability to accomplish what Hebrews 4:12 speaks of than I ever knew when I first heard it as a twenty-five year old.

3. A helpful treatment of this is **Sitting at the Feet of Rabbi Jesus** by Ann Spangler.

Note: I am grateful for Ron J's book **Impossible Joy,** which forms much of the basis for this booklet. I highly recommend this book for those facing sexual addiction issues and its important message of addressing lust, like Jesus did as the core issue, rather than the behaviors it leads to.

Made in the USA
Middletown, DE
23 September 2021